Connect, Build, Grow

How to Build Relationships and Grow Your Network

ASHLEY RENÉ CASEY

Back-Pocket Business Guide: Volume 1

Copyright © 2016 Ashley René Casey

The quoted ideas expressed in this book were discovered using internet search engines.

All Rights Reserved. No part of this book may be reproduced, disseminated or utilized in any form without permission from the author.

Requests for permission to make copies of any part of the work should be submitted to the author by emailing:

info@beboldandspeak.com

Original and modified cover art by NaCDS and CoverDesignStudio.com

Book edited by Amanda Foster

Be Bold and Speak Logo designed by JadeBerth Creative

To Miles and Langston. I love and appreciate you both, more than you will ever know.

To my mom. I would not be where I am today without your love and tireless support.

To my friends. Thank you for the encouragement to pursue this project.

TABLE OF CONTENTS

NETWORKING, THE MISUNDERSTOOD BUSINESS TOOL — III

CHAPTER 1: NETWORKING 101 – WHAT NETWORKING IS, WHAT NETWORKING ISN'T — 1

CHAPTER 2: BE INTENTIONAL – KNOW YOUR WHY — 5

CHAPTER 3: KNOW YOUR NETWORK – EVALUATING CURRENT RELATIONSHIPS — 13

CHAPTER 4: KNOW YOUR PRESENCE – EVALUATING YOUR BRAND — 23

CHAPTER 5: KNOW YOUR PRESENTATION – EVALUATING YOUR TALENT — 39

CHAPTER 6: MEETING POTENTIAL STRATEGIC PARTNERS   51

CHAPTER 7: ENGAGING STRATEGIC PARTNERS   63

CHAPTER 8: MAINTAINING YOUR RELATIONSHIPS   73

CHAPTER 9: NETWORKING NUGGETS   75

Networking, the Misunderstood Business Tool

Although we have likely never met one another, I like you already. You probably picked up this book because you have goals. Maybe you have a corporate job and want to take it to the next level. Maybe you own a business and want to see it grow. Maybe you are about to graduate college and want to be ahead of the game. Maybe you are someone simply seeking a new way to build relationships. Whatever your reason, I respect it.

Networking tends to be one of those rituals many people despise. They find it uncomfortable talking to people they do not know. They feel awkward guiding a conversation. And even though building a solid network is essential, most people would rather play it safe with the people they already know.

What if I told you that I could help reduce the anxiety felt around the thought of networking? What if I told you I could make networking fun? That is my goal in this book. I want to help remove the barriers that have been created around the idea of networking. The first barrier is the word "networking."

The term "networking" has a contrived and manipulative reputation. Networking does not traditionally give you a warm feeling. From here out, I want you to think of "networking" as "building relationships." When we build relationships, we are building mutual avenues for success and assistance. That is networking.

When you finish reading this book, and completing the assessments found throughout, you will be ready to connect with others, build relationships and grow your network. In addition, you will have clarity towards your goals so you can properly leverage your time, your talent and your people.

Chapter 1: Networking 101 – What Networking Is, What Networking Isn't

"You can get everything in life you want, if you help enough other people get what they want." –Zig Ziglar

When I lead classes on networking I often open by asking participants what they think of when they think about networking. Some people react with a smile and a verbal response of "an opportunity." Those are typically the extroverts. Then, from the opposite side of the room another participant sharply, without hesitation, states, "No, networking gives me anxiety – I hate it!"

Networking is one of those things that riles some people up into pure joy and excitement (I fall into that camp) while simultaneously winding others into knots. When we do a little probing, we find out those who would rather get a root canal typically have one thing in common: they are uncomfortable meeting new people.

There are many reasons why meeting new people can be uncomfortable. *Will they like me? Will I have anything to offer? Will they find me interesting? Will we have anything in common? Will we have anything to talk about?* I guarantee you, with the right mindset you can talk with anyone about anything with confidence and ease. What type of mindset affords that? An open mindset that is willing to serve.

To effectively build relationships we must be open to new ideas, new perspectives and new possibilities. Given how connected we are as a society, you never know where a conversation might lead.

Not only must we be open to new ideas, new perspectives and new possibilities, but we must also be open to the idea that we have something valuable to offer, no matter who we speak with. Our experiences, both personal and professional, are valuable and worthy to be shared. When we connect with one another, we are also offering our talents and abilities.

Once we have the proper mindset we can then begin to dissect what networking is and what networking isn't. If you read the intro you will remember that the term "networking" is not my favorite term, instead I prefer the phrase "building relationships." Building relationships inherently offers a give and take. When we build relationships, we are actively participating and contributing to its strength. We are adding value with our knowledge, talents, gifts, time, money, connections and more. If you are approaching new people with a "what's in it for me" attitude, you are going about it all wrong. Strong networks are built with mutually beneficial, solid relationships.

Know that building relationships takes time and effort. Just like most people do not get married the first day they meet, you will likely not be able to call someone a member of your network the first day you meet them. Be patient with yourself, practice process and allow your relationships to grow.

The next sections of this book will offer a step by step process of how to build solid relationships and, in turn a dynamic, robust network. Take advantage of the self-assessments. Be honest with yourself as you answer and be open to feeling comfortably uncomfortable. Remember, networking is more than shaking hands, it's connecting to people and building a relationship. It's adding value and serving others.

Takeaways and Recap

- Having an open mind and acknowledging how you will serve the relationship is the first step to building solid relationships.
- Solid networks are built with mutually beneficial, solid relationships.
- Relationships are a give and take.
- Relationships (and networks) take time and effort to build.
- Networking is more than shaking hands, it's connecting to people and building relationships.

Chapter 2: Be Intentional – Know Your Why

"Efforts and courage are not enough without purpose and direction." –John F. Kennedy

Like anything else you do in life, building your network must be done with purpose. Knowing why you made the decision to attend an event will help keep you motivated. Knowing the specific type of person you would like to build a relationship with will help guide you to who you will have conversations with. Think of it this way: you would not apply for jobs you could not serve with your talents; why would you attend an event or speak with people you could not serve?

This is not a cop-out to not attend events or approach people, rather it is a way to remind you that your network of relationships should and can be built strategically. It is meant for you to pay close attention to your activities and conversations. Are you carefully handling situations that could prove pivotal to your success?

I vividly remember working at a major corporation, moving from field operations to working at the corporate office. I was extremely excited to dive right into everything corporate had to offer. There were development workshops, networking events, affinity groups, galas that were corporately sponsored – as a social butterfly I was in heaven. I attended every event I could. I met everyone I could. I was active. I was involved. I was busy.

My heart was full because I had always dreamed of attending these types of events. Development workshops made me feel valued as an employee. Networking events made me feel like I was going to meet someone and knock them out of their socks with how awesome I was. Galas were my favorite. I dressed up in beautiful gowns and rubbed elbows with other people who were dressed up.

Eventually I stopped, took a step back and realized that I had built not one meaningful relationship. I spent lots of time talking with people but not a lot of time determining how I could serve them or how to create a mutually beneficial relationship. I flitted from event to event but took back nothing but memories and programs. Now some of my memories are very rich and meaningful, so for that I am thankful; however, one would assume that by attending these events I would have gained a wide range of contacts.

I was not intentional. I was not seeking to serve others. I attended events without purpose.

If I had known the importance of being intentional when attending events, I would have collected a wider range of contacts. Years later I got it and began moving with purpose, but if I had gotten it earlier who knows how different things could have been.

You see, being intentional is not just about having a goal in mind with who you speak with and where you go. When you are intentional you create a boundary for your time and your energy. Given that each of us only have 24 hours in a day, we must be smart with how we spend it. We do not lack time, but it is limited – spend it wisely.

Thinking back to my experience when I transitioned to corporate, the time I spent at events that did not add true value could have been spent working on a meaningful project or even spending quality time with my children. **Know your why, work your why and honor it.**

Will every event bring a new relationship? No. Will every event bring a new experience? Yes. If you attend an event with purpose and that purpose is not fulfilled, find at least 3 things you did take away. Maybe you have a nice outfit now because of the event. Perhaps you had a chance to laugh with someone. You could have possibly learned something new. Be intentional but do not be dismayed if your goal is not met.

So how do you determine your intent? How do you build your goal? How do you know your why?

Complete the statements below.

My current position today is:

___

In five years I want to be:

___

The skills I currently possess are:

___

The skills I will need to reach my goals are:

___
___

These may seem like basic statements but they are the purest elements to your why. Although you might be seeking someone to have in your network for your next position, having your slightly longer-term goals in mind will help you maneuver strategically. Also, being aware of what you currently possess and what you need will give you confidence in knowing what you bring to the table and what you are seeking help with.

Once you are clear on where you are now and where you want to be, ask yourself:

Will this event contribute to my goals? Will I be able to connect with someone whom I can serve and in turn be served?

Do not start turning down invitations to events simply because they do not move you forward in your goals. Life is meant to be enjoyed so by all means hang out with friends, bring your family to new places, attend events to support friends, have fun. However, be aware of when you are attending an event for fun and when you are attending an event to build relationships for your network.

You have made the decision that attending a specific event is worthwhile for building relationships. Now it's time to approach others. Be brave. Strike up conversations with people who you do not know. We will go into further detail about how to engage with others but at this point you must realize that you are attending an event for a purpose, or approaching someone with a goal in mind. You are being intentional.

Your success in life has grown because you have set goals and made strides towards those goals. Building your network is no different than your approach to other areas in your life. Set goals for yourself. Know why you are attending an event. Understand your motives behind reaching out or speaking to someone. Being intentional with where you go, what you do and who you connect with is not selfish, it is you honoring your time so it is spent wisely.

Takeaways and Recap

- Build relationships with purpose.
- Know where you are and where you want to be.
- Know what you have and what you need.
- Understand the difference between attending an event with the intent to build and the intent to have fun.
- Being intentional not only guides your actions but it also guards your time – <u>time is your most precious commodity.</u>

Connect, Build, Grow

Chapter 3: Know Your Network – Evaluating Current Relationships

"To succeed in this world you have to be known to people." –Sonia Sotomayor

Being intentional as we build our network helps us to stay focused on our goals. It guides our actions. But how will you know where to make the connections if you don't know what connections you already have and which connections you are lacking?

You are likely familiar with those in your network who you consider yourself to be close with. You could probably identify a major connector in your network (they are the gregarious ones who never meet a stranger). And although you can identify these individuals, you probably have never taken an inventory of the people you know. Honestly, it is not a natural thing to do, but neither is listing all the jobs we have held. Keeping a solid list of who is in our network is a good way to measure how close we are to our goals.

It feels good to be able to quickly recall someone. However we miss other opportunities by not keeping track of who we know. This doesn't mean making a list of everyone you know, but keep a list of those people in your network you want to stay engaged with. As we will discuss later, connecting with people when we do not need them is critical if we are genuinely building relationships.

Go ahead and list the top 10 people in your network. Write down the person's name, their title, where they work, what role they play in your network and how you met them. Examples of different roles someone can play within your network include sharing wisdom, being a sounding board, accountability, mentoring (mentor or mentee), financial guidance, spiritual guidance, connector, glean leadership style, etc.

Here are a few examples to guide you.

Jazmin Peters, Accountant, Zane and Barnes Consulting, Business Tips – met at industry conference

Chase Archer, Regional Director of Operations, GFE Manufacturing, Sounding Board – introduced by mutual friend

James Sanders, Sr Analyst of Market Research, Worldwide Widget Solutions, my mentee – met in lobby at work

Etta Chaney, AVP Customer Support, International Telatronics, exemplary leader – former boss

My Top 10 (Go To)

1.

2.

3.

4.

5.

6.

7.

8.

9.

10.

Now review who is in your "go to" list. Is it diverse? Do you have people you can go to for a variety of things? Do you have people from various industries?

A good network is diverse and rich with variety. It is built with people from various industries, various backgrounds and various educational experiences. Why? Because you can learn more through diversity. The more naturally diverse your network is, the more diverse your experiences and opportunities will be.

Viewing your network and how it helps you is important; however, equally important is viewing your network and recognizing how everyone within it is potentially served. Your diverse network will afford you the opportunity to connect others. You might have a college student in your network because you are mentoring them. You also might have an HR Hiring Manager who works at a company that the college student is interested in. Because you made it a point to have a diverse network you can connect the college student and the HR Hiring Manager. You are able to serve others and add value.

Diversity is not just good for a company's bottom line, it is good for yours as well.

You are your own business, even if you work for someone else. You are responsible for your success. If you have people within your network who all work within the same industry and the industry is suddenly shaken, where will you go? Or if you have people in your network who all possess the same level of education and hold the same types of positions, when you are ready to promote, who will you turn to? You want options. Do not be afraid to seek different. Different is good.

Along the same lines, be sure your network has people who work outside of the company you currently work for. You might have people from different backgrounds, various degrees of education and who hold a variety of positions – but they all work at the same company you do. This is a very common mistake people make. It is easy to do given that we spend more time with the people we work with than our own family.

However, in a world where markets are dynamic and new technologies disrupt business models rapidly, companies must be agile. Sometimes this means laying employees off and right sizing more frequently. As unsettling as this all is, these actions are necessary if a company wants to stay competitive and keep its doors open. I guarantee you that leaders are looking at all options before they disrupt a person's livelihood. The decision to layoff or abolish a position is not one that is done lightly.

As painful as a layoff can be, those who are most protected in the face of a layoff are those who can reach out to their robust network for support. If all your connections are internal and your company must downsize, where will you go? Who will you turn to if all your contacts are at that company? The environment we live in hosts a large selection of very well educated workers. We no longer compete based upon our talents but rather we compete based upon who knows us. Who knows you?

Traditionally people have said "it's not what you know but who you know." I want you to challenge this notion. You might very well "know" someone but if they do not know you then the relationship lacks real meaning. When it comes down to reaching out to someone when you need them, say after being laid off, will they have to think back to when they met you? This is where building relationships is so incredibly important. People will work with who they know and who they trust.

Use the space below and list 5 people you need in your network. Maybe you have a specific person in mind you have been meaning to connect with. Perhaps you need a specific type of person – someone in a certain industry or someone with a certain quality. Another way I like to do this exercise, pick a person who seems completely out of reach (a celebrity, an executive, a politician) and list them. If you have goals to be at that level one day, you will want someone at that level in your "go to" list.

My Top 5 (I want in my network)

1.
2.
3.
4.
5.

A successful network is one that is diverse. A successful network is one where people are connected to a variety of opportunities. Be aware of how your network is built. Do you have people who represent a variety of experiences, connections, opportunities, wisdom, knowledge?

As you build your network you will also be building relationships, but you need to know what kind of relationships you currently have and what kind of relationships you need. Take an inventory of your network at least twice a year. I recommend January and September. At the beginning of the year people are executing annual plans and beginning to work towards their goals. By September, people are beginning to think about their plans for the following year. When you go through your inventory and you check in with the people on your list, you increase your visibility and the possibility to be included in their plans.

Takeaways and Recap

- A solid network is diverse.
- A diverse network reduces risk and increases possibility.
- Know who your "go-to" people are.
- Know who you need to add to make your network more diverse and robust.
- Inventory your network at least twice a year.

Connect, Build, Grow

Chapter 4: Know Your Presence – Evaluating Your Brand

"You are the chief marketing officer for the brand called you, but what others say about your brand is more impactful than what you say about yourself." – Dan Schawbel

The idea that companies needed to brand themselves came about in the mid-1950s. Company branding gave customers something to relate their experience to. Catchy phrases and memorable logos helped build loyalty around everything from cigarettes to soap to cars.

Today, more than ever, companies rely on branding to create a following and evoke visceral feelings around their company. When we think about Dove soap we might start to feel good about ourselves because a major part of their ad campaigns focus on positive self-image, with the tag line "Every Body is Beautiful." When we think of Coca-Cola, we might hear the release of fizz even with no can around because Coca-Cola has done a good job of including that sound in much of their advertising with the tag line "Taste the Feeling."

Branding is a powerful tool that companies use. You are no different. The feeling you evoke when people think about you is equally important to the quality of work you produce. As mentioned in previous sections of this book, talent is abundant, employers have no problem finding qualified applicants. What employers are looking for are people who align with their company culture and mission. They want to know that who they hire will fit in.

Without even trying, you have a brand. People have a perceived notion about who you are by how you show up. From how you dress to how you speak to the work you have produced, you have a personal brand.

As we cultivate relationships to build our network, it is important to recognize our brand. What type of feelings do you evoke when people meet you? Do you come across as knowledgeable? Do you come across as friendly? Do you come across as fun? Do you come across as approachable?

This kind of awareness requires an acute openness to hearing feedback from others and taking inventory of yourself. Before we go any further, you need to know that being you is the most important thing you can be. Do not attempt to be someone you are not. You can absolutely be a better version of yourself but the moment you start changing the essence of who you are, you will fall apart. People need to like you for who you are; if they don't, then you don't need them.

Let's look at the components that make up a personal brand: your image, your message and your attitude.

YOUR IMAGE

People are very visual creatures. We make snap judgements based upon what we see. Before someone speaks we judge their mental abilities, their social status, their knowledge. Do we sometimes get it wrong? Absolutely. Is this something we should be aware of? Most definitely!

If appearances did not matter, there would not be thousands of books and articles written about how to dress for an interview or what to wear on a first date. If two men both have neat haircuts but one man is dressed in khaki pants and a polo shirt and the other is dressed in a suit, we would likely rate the intelligence of the man in the suit as higher. A woman wearing a tailored pencil skirt and blazer will be regarded as having more power than a woman wearing an A-line skirt and cardigan sweater.

The image we project is one of the most important pieces to building our personal brand. To attract quality people into your network you must appear to be a quality prospect. Here are few tips regarding attire that apply to both males and females:

- <u>Wear clothes that fit</u>. If you have lost weight, congratulate yourself and purchase clothes that fit. If you are on the other side of the coin and have gained weight, purchase clothes that fit until you reach your desired goal weight. Clothes should complement your shape; ill- fitting clothes detract and distract.
- <u>Wear clothes that are neatly pressed, without wrinkles</u>. Wrinkles show a lack of pride in your appearance and could potentially be perceived as a lack of pride in your work. Take the extra time to iron your clothes. If you do not have the extra time but are willing to spend the extra money, take your clothes to the cleaners.
- <u>Wear clothes/shoes without tears or holes</u>. This should go without saying but I see it often (and

I've been guilty of it). It is your favorite shirt or favorite pair of shoes – patch it or get rid of it. Our eyes are drawn to inconsistency. When there is a hole or tear in an article of clothing, we become distracted by the inconsistency and stop paying attention to the person.

- <u>Wear clothes that fit the occasion</u>. What you wear to an interview you would likely not wear to a baseball game and vice versa. Dress for the occasion. If you are unsure what the dress code is, ask. When in doubt, overdress. The worst thing that can happen when you overdress is that you are uncomfortable, but everyone else will wonder "Who is that?"
- <u>Wear clothes that fit your body type</u>. This is a tricky one. If you cannot tell on your own what lines fit your body and which lines do not, ask someone. This mostly applies to women; however, men's clothing has evolved over the years and not every style is flattering to every body type.
- <u>Wear colors that complement you</u>. This too is tricky and might require professional assistance or a good friend with an eye for color. Although anyone can wear any color, there are certain colors that look better on people with certain skin tones,

eye color and hair color. Learn what your colors are and build your wardrobe around those colors.
- <u>Wear accessories with confidence</u>. We have entered a new era with accessories. Know the culture and expectations of the place you are going. I have seen men in suits wearing rubber bracelets for their kids' basketball team and no one batted an eye. Whatever you do, if you wear an accessory, wear it with confidence.

Clothing is very a personal thing. Clothing can also be a very expensive thing. And unfortunately, clothing is the first thing people see. If you are not in a financial position to purchase clothes you would like, look for sales. You can also spread your purchases out and buy one new item each pay period. You will be surprised at how quickly your wardrobe will grow using this approach.

Buy essential, classic pieces that can be mixed and matched throughout the year. Be consistent and stay true to what you feel comfortable in. Don't buy a bold print if that is not who you are. If you don't feel comfortable in bright colors, leave them on the rack.

You will lack confidence if you feel uncomfortable in what you are wearing.

Another aspect of your image to consider is personal grooming. I will never forget straightening my hair and people I saw everyday did not recognize me. For me, my curly hair is a critical part of my brand. People identify me with my hair. Although I laughed each time someone did a double take, it drove home the point on the power of our personal brand. Other grooming items to consider: facial hair, odor, makeup and fingernails.

You may have never considered the impact of your image to your network, but what people see determines whether they will want to connect Have a conversation with someone you trust. Learn where your opportunities exist. Invest in yourself. Look the part until you get the part.

YOUR MESSAGE

The branding of yourself as it relates to your message is what you say and how you say it. What is it that you stand for? How do you express what you stand for?

Let's first examine what you stand for, your values.

We all carry a different set of values. Our upbringing and our experiences throughout life have colored the lens through which we view life. Religion, social status, family make-up, educational level – each of these impact us in different ways. Someone who grew up in the small town of Paris, Texas, is going to approach life differently than someone who grew up in the big city of Paris, France.

There is no approach to life that is right or wrong, each approach just is. As we build our network, it is important to be aware of this and keep an open mind. Remaining open to a variety of values towards life presents opportunities you may have never known to exist. Not to mention, you want others to be open to you and your values.

Be aware of what you value and of how you view the world. Although our message is not typically revealed until we engage in conversation, people quickly hone in on what others value. Our values tend to steer conversation. Our values tend to drive our decisions. What is that you value? What drives your intentions? How does this show up in your message?

In this same thread is the delivery – how we express ourselves, how we deliver our message. Each of us has a unique speech patterns. For most of us it is based on where we were born and how we were raised. (There is a theme here.)

The delivery of our message is defined by our body language and our speech pattern. What is your default posture? Do you have certain words that you say often? Are there certain parts of speech that you inflect in a way that is unique?

To drive this home, think about the following people and specifically recall how their speech patterns and demeanor. Sylvester Stallone. Dolly Parton. Christopher Walken. Angela Bassett. Jennifer Lopez. Michael Jackson. Betty White. Elizabeth Taylor. Martin Luther King Jr. President Barack Obama. President George W. Bush.

Each of these public figures has (or had) very distinct voices. They have signature stances and take up space in a way that is memorable. Whether you like them or not, you could probably pick them out in a room or over the phone. This is the power of our verbal and non-verbal communication.

Although I grew up in Texas, I did not grow up with a Southern accent. Southern manners, yes, but no accent. In fact, my mother was quite adamant about our diction and posture. She insisted that we sit up straight and project proper diction. As a result of this stringent approach, I pronounce nearly every "t" in every word. Additionally, my default posture is shoulders back, back straight. Both habits have been pointed out to me throughout my life. They have nothing to do with me "trying" to be a certain way, it's just how I am. Over the years I have learned that these traits leave an impression on people and make them feel a certain way. Having this awareness has helped me flex and leverage in ways I would not have before had I not taken a step back to objectively observe my message.

Your message is a combination of your values and your expressions. Knowing how your values and expressions make others feel is a part of your presence and your brand. After they see you, they hear you. Be perceptive to this. For example, you might be quite amiable but you speak loudly and when it is on a subject you are passionate about, you become even louder and appear abrasive. Of course, that wasn't your intent but it is the message that is received.

Know your message. Know what you stand for. Know what is important to you and do not be ashamed of it. Your values are a part of who you are. They guide your decisions and show up in your daily life. Be clear how your message comes across. Be sure that your verbal and non-verbal communication is consistent with what matters most to you. If someone is going to vouch for you, they need know who you are – your message reveals this.

YOUR ATTITUDE

Maya Angelou said it best, "People will forget what you said, people will forget what you did, but people will never forget how made them feel." The attitude you choose impacts how people feel. Not how well you are educated, not how much money you have, not the titles you hold, not even where you are from.

Many people might initially be impressed by material things and moved by status, but those are not the things that keep them. If you are serious about building solid relationships and solid networks, you will want to examine your attitude.

Your attitude is the glue that will hold a relationship together. When there is a choice between two highly qualified candidates with the exact experience and credentials, the candidate with the better attitude will be hired 9 out of 10 times.

Oxford Dictionary defines attitude as "a settled way of thinking or feeling about someone or something, typically one that is reflected in a person's behavior." Think about that. You do not have to say anything for your attitude to be detected. Your attitude shows up in your behavior.

Some people dismiss the idea of mindset, but this is where mindset plays a critical role in our success, as our thoughts are revealed by our behavior. If we hold negative ideas, our actions will mimic the ideas even if we do not intend for them to. We might try to conceal but water only boils so long before it lets off steam.

Why is this important? Life is too short and people do not want to add stress to their lives with negativity. Think about your current environment. I am sure there is at least one person who you know to be a downer. They complain about everything. They criticize everyone. Instead of seeing the silver lining, they focus on the rain. Most likely, you feel drained when you speak with them. You may even avoid them. Do you see the damage this person is doing to themselves? They have reduced their opportunities because of their attitude.

Add value to those around you by being amiable. Be a light with your words. Smile. Compliment others. Be kind. Serve. Talk about the bright spots. Acknowledge success. Be a tough-minded optimist. Have a positive attitude. Be the one people want to be around because you make them feel good.

You relate to products because of their quality but you are loyal to a product because of its brand. When people make the decision to build a relationship with you, they are choosing to build a relationship because you not only produce quality work but because you also have a quality brand.

Complete the statements in the next section. Because you only see certain parts of yourself, find someone who can provide you with open feedback. Knowing your trade elevates earnings. Knowing yourself elevates your capacity for success.

When they see me, what do they see? (What is your style? What is their first impression? Approachable? Competitive? Light-hearted? Smart? Wise? Friendly? Animated? Leader? Serious?)

_____

_____

_____

_____

_____

When they hear my name, what do they think? (Is my mission clear? Is my vision clear? Are my skills recognized? Am I aligned?)

_____

_____

_____

_____

_____

When they see me and when they hear me I want them to think and feel…

_____
_____
_____
_____
_____
_____
_____
_____
_____

Know your brand. Take inventory often to see if actual perceptions align with your desired perceptions. Be open to hearing what others say about your presence. Be willing to change what needs to be changed so you articulate your vision clearly when people meet you.

TAKEAWAYS AND RECAP

- How you are perceived will determine how you are received – have a brand that is well received.
- Your image, your message and your attitude make up the three main components of your brand.
- People notice inconsistencies. Wear clothes that accent your personality and always be true to you.
- People will forget what you say and what you did but they will not forget how you made them feel.
- Self-assess how you are perceived but also seek honest feedback from someone you trust.

Chapter 5: Know Your Presentation – Evaluating Your Talent

"Hide not your talents, they for use were made. What's a sundial in the shade?" – **Benjamin Franklin**

You are good at something. In fact, you might even be the best at something. You have a talent that you have developed over the years and you are proud of it. Does anyone know what your something is? Do they acknowledge you as the go-to person?

Selling our talents can be uncomfortable. Our culture teaches us to be modest and play small so that we do not make others feel uncomfortable. Although modesty is admirable, there is a way to share what you do while honoring your hard work and letting others know that you are highly capable and qualified.

Basketball legend Hakeem Abdul Olajuwon once said "When you get to that level, it's not a matter of talent anymore – because all the players are so talented – it's about preparation, about playing smart and making good decisions."

We live in a time where college degrees are common place. More people hold graduate degrees than ever before. You likely work at a company or in an industry where everyone is degreed. The individuals who stand out among the sea of talent are those who are prepared and able to articulate what they bring to the table. They are the ones who know exactly what to say to stand out. They are the ones who leave an impression on those they speak with because they are prepared.

Your elevator speech, or pitch, is the opportunity for you to share how amazing you are. In a not so subtle way it gives insight to why someone should build a relationship with you. It is the compelling (and concise) story you tell to sell you. It is your opportunity to express "Why you?"

I have seen many incredibly talented people get the pitch wrong. One way this is accomplished is robotically. They approach the pitch without showing personality. Like a business hostage, they give their name, rattle off the company they work for and the title they hold. Sadly unaware, they are come off as dull and not memorable at all.

Conversely, some people share their entire work history since high school, including that amazing summer gig as a lifeguard. Whether it is because they think every position matters or they are nervous and not paying attention remains unclear. Unfortunately, they say a lot without saying anything worth remembering.

Your pitch needs to answer the following:

1. **Who** you are.
2. **What** you do.
3. **How** you serve.

Answer those three things in way that that is engaging, likable and memorable and you will spark interest. Keep it simple enough that an eight-year-old and eighty-year-old will understand. Refrain from using jargon and confusing statements. Remember, people do business with people they know and trust. If you complicate your message you will alienate yourself.

Answer the following questions with one to two sentences:

What is your job title and where do you work? (If you are seeking employment, what field are seeking employment in?)

_____

_____

How do you add value to your company? (This answer should add meaning to the title you hold and express your capabilities in acting and adding value.)

_____

_____

_____

_____

How do you add value to the greater good? (This answer provides the impact your work has on a more global scale. How does your work influence your immediate community? How does your work influence how others live?)

_____

_____

_____

_____

Keep your pitch short and to the point. Remember, the idea of an elevator pitch is to sell your product – in this case yourself – during the time it would take to ride an elevator: around 30-60 seconds. This is not a lot of time so the more concise your message, the more impact you will have.

You have already learned to manage your personal brand from the previous section of this book but you must be able to follow up with a personal pitch. What makes you amazing? What is it about you that will make them want to do business with you in the future? What is about you that stands out among the other people in the room, or in the elevator?

The nature of your pitch will vary slightly when you are in a situation where you have more time. This does not mean you go into your history but it does mean that you will need to have more material to talk about. At the end of this chapter you will find a space to list potential conversation topics.

Because people do business with people, share **something professional, something personal** and **something unique**. This approach helps to lay a solid foundation to begin building a relationship.

PROFESSIONAL

You are used to sharing professional information about yourself: projects you have been a part of, fascinating positions you have held, companies you have worked for that contributed to your growth and successes you have experienced in your career.

Be sure that whatever professional information you share is relevant. The other person should hear your message and think "How can I fit them into my plans?" or "How can I help them?"

Know who it is you are talking with. If they are in your industry, establish yourself as an expert and speak the language. If they are not, then keep it simple. This goes with the territory of being prepared – know your audience.

Do not be afraid to share your professional goals, but use discretion. Casual mention of your goals is typically safe; however, you will turn the listener off if you only talk about what you want, especially if it is a promotion or specific position. People need to know you and like you before they can start making moves for you. Take your cues from the setting and the person you are speaking with.

PERSONAL

Getting personal with someone is often our biggest struggle. There is negative judgement that can sometimes happen when we get personal. Stay above the line and share those items that are not controversial: marital status, children, where you are from, activities you are involved in outside of work.

Being vulnerable and sharing something personal will move you forward faster in the process of building a relationship. Sharing something personal does not mean laying out all your deepest secrets. On the contrary, it is revealing to others that you are more than a title.

Think about it. Would you want to work with someone who only talks about work? Sometimes we need an escape from work – even while we are at work! People will want to be around you if you can be that escape.

Typically, after you share, the person you are speaking with will also share. Be sure you are respectful. Genuinely listen to what they say and take note. Remember, getting personal is a big thing. Don't be the reason why they keep their guard up.

UNIQUE

Of the billions of people on the planet, there is no one like you. There may be people who share the same name or bear a striking resemblance, but you are the only one. Wear that with pride.

Unique experiences come in many shapes and sizes. They are typically things you do not commonly find. They can fall under the professional or personal categories When people hear an interesting and unique story, their ears perk up and they are captivated.

Maybe you are an avid scuba diver. Perhaps you have competed on a reality game show. It could be that you were the creative mind behind a game-changing process or tool. Whatever it is, few people have ever done and because of that, those of us who have never done it want to know more.

The key to sharing something unique is to tell a good story because who you are speaking with will likely want to know more. Be energetic. Use colorful adjectives. Move your body. Bring them into the experience.

Here is an example of what a quick pitch might look like:

Hi! My name is Latrice Johnson. I have been a Registered Nurse at Central Hospital for almost 10 years. I always knew I wanted to be a nurse, so to live my dream has been amazing. When I'm not at the hospital though I love camping. Work hard, play hard!

Another example:

Nice to meet you. I am Thomas Noel. I have served in the United States Navy for the past 6 years as an Aviation Mechanic. I recently ended my contract and have been seeking the next big thing. I enjoyed the adventure the Navy offered but I also really enjoyed the challenges that were brought each day. I am not originally from this area but I am loving it. I have already found a place to practice archery.

Be concise, be positive and hit the highlights. Be prepared to offer your business card or an alternate way to connect later.

Getting your pitch down pat will take practice. Stand in front of a mirror and practice. You can also use your cell phone and record yourself. Is your energy attractive? Is your stance inviting? Are you speaking at a reasonable pace? Is your message concise and easy to understand? Are you engaging?

Use the chart below to list at least 3 highlights you would feel comfortable sharing with a stranger. Always have a base pitch but mix it up occasionally. Have more to talk about if the conversation is longer than 30-60 seconds.

Professional

Personal

Unique

TAKEAWAYS AND RECAP

- Be prepared. Articulate the value you bring.
- Your pitch answers "Who you are," "What you do," and "Why you matter."
- Your pitch should be stated within 30-60 second.
- A memorable pitch will share something <u>professional</u>, something <u>personal</u> and something <u>unique</u>.
- Stand in front of a mirror or record yourself to gauge the impact of your pitch.

Connect, Build, Grow

Chapter 6: Meeting Potential Strategic Partners

"An entrepreneur needs to know what they need, period. Then they need to find an investor who can build off whatever their weaknesses are – whether that's through money, strategic partnerships or knowledge." – Daymond John

The world that we live in knows few barriers for connecting with others. Favorite celebrity has a Twitter account? Tweet at them. Have an opinion about a new work policy? Email HR. Thinking about that old high school flame? Google them.

Our abilities to connect with new people have expanded drastically with the internet. We are no longer tied to the network of people within our town. Of course, traditional face-to-face connection is still relevant and highly sought after.

Regardless of which method you use to build relationships, know that you have options. **Your willingness to explore new avenues for connecting will determine your success.**

As you continue reading, think back to the list of individuals you would like to add to your network. Where do they hang out? What do they do when they are not at work? Are there activities they are known to participate in? Are there organizations they are already connected with? Understand how they move and move accordingly.

CONNECTING IN PERSON

Although technology is amazing, reality is better. There is something about looking someone in their eyes and shaking their hand. You can't replicate the feeling of sharing a meal with someone through wireless data connections. And stories just don't read the same way electronically as they do in person. It is easier for us to detect an individual's character and personality when we connect in person.

One easy way to build a relationship with someone is to invite them out for a drink or a meal. It is said that more deals are made this way than in offices and meeting rooms. Lunch and coffee are great for first meetings. If you are already familiar with the person, then dinner or drinks is acceptable. Take advantage of the opportunity to connect in person and focus on building a genuine bond. Remember your "why" but also use the more casual atmosphere to really get to know the other person.

Maybe you are not ready for one-on-one meet ups. That is ok. You might consider finding fun, organized events with many people instead. Seek activities where there will be people who share your same values and respect your goals.

Galas, networking parties, kick-off events, store openings, meet-ups and conferences offer a fun way to connect with a diverse group of people. If your company will pay for you to attend a conference, I highly recommend taking advantage of it. Conferences serve a dual purpose of learning and meeting new people. They can be costly but they are well worth it.

Leverage your current network to discover events near you. Ask people in your current network if there are things going on that you could attend. By leveraging your current network, you remain relevant and engaging in the relationship. You want to take advantage of any opportunity available to you to strengthen your current relationships.

Apps like Meetup and Eventbrite also serve as excellent ways to find out what is happening. Meetup and Eventbrite are both free apps that you can download from the Apple or Android app store (neither are available through Microsoft).

As the name suggests, Meetup is an app that people use to form groups who share a common interest and then meet up. I have used this app before and have met incredible people that I am still friends with years later. Groups on the app range from special interest such as people who enjoy singing karaoke, to more professional groups such as people who are entrepreneurs. If you do not see a group that meets your needs, start your own.

Eventbrite focuses specifically on planned events. Some events are small while others are quite large. Just like Meetup, the events that are posted range in what they offer. I have seen many conferences posted onto Eventbrite, as well as unique events like independent movie screenings.

Be aware that both apps cater to bigger cities. If you live in a small town, you might not find anything. However, if you live in a bigger city I highly recommend downloading at least one and browsing what is available near you.

If the idea of getting spruced up turns you off, then you might consider volunteering. Volunteering is a wonderful way to build new relationships and serve the community you live in. Non-profit organization are usually always in need of volunteers. Go online and browse the website of a local non-profit to learn about upcoming opportunities. A servant heart is always rewarded. The reward might not be seen immediately but it will be seen.

Once you find an organization you want to serve, begin serving and consistently show up. The more you show up the more you expose yourself to individuals you can meaningfully connect with. As someone who does like to dress up, I enjoy the fundraising events that the non-profits host. Not only is it fun to dress up but there are often people who share the same desire of success at fundraising events. Fundraising events are typically not cheap, but if your goal is to connect with someone with clout, it is worth the investment.

Finally, do not underestimate fun, common spaces and events. Waiting in line to check out? Strike a conversation. Have children? Join the PTA. Avid fitness buff? Participate in an endurance event or competition. Attend a house of worship? Get involved with a ministry. If there is a professional group for the industry you work, join.

People tend to have the guards down when they are just doing life (as opposed to striving towards a goal). These types of non-threatening environments are the best for genuine, meaningful relationships. There might be a small fee associated for participating, but at least you know that you have something in common with everyone else.

There are many real-life opportunities available for growing your network. Ge up, get out and take advantage of them.

CONNECTING ONLINE

The internet: a modern day "Wild West." With few rules for engagement, the possibilities are nearly endless for building relationships. Social media platforms, website forums and traditional email contact give us options.

A simple way to grow your network is to find online groups to join. Both LinkedIn and Facebook have common interest groups that anyone can join. Interest groups can be both social and professional. After you join the group, engage. Read posts and provide insight in the comments section. Share posts and reply to comments that other people leave. This type of engagement helps people see where your mind is. They could very well read your contributions and reach out to you to connect. Join a group and engage.

Below is a list of the top social media sites to connect with people. Each is utilized differently and have unique functions. Recall what your intentions are, figure out which tool you are most comfortable with and jump right in. If you can manage two, then go for two.

LinkedIn

A professional social media platform, LinkedIn is a great way to showcase your experience while also directly connecting with others in your industry. Position yourself as an expert by sharing relevant posts. Follow and connect with both peers and leaders in your field. Engage by commenting on their posts.

Endorse the skills of those you know. If you direct message someone, be sure to acknowledge their expertise or express appreciation for what they have accomplished before making a request. Also, take advantage of the professional groups on LinkedIn. Good information is usually shared in LinkedIn groups.

Facebook

The original major social media platform: Facebook. Although Facebook is more of a place to share personal stories, there are many opportunities to make connections. Joining groups on Facebook has become one of the fastest ways to build new relationships with people who share a common interest. When you discover a group, take time to engage in posts. As you begin to engage, people will go to you. With over one billion users, I guarantee there is at least one person you can build a solid relationship with on Facebook.

Twitter

Twitter is an interesting social media platform. Users are limited to only 140 character posts and utilize hashtags to join in on trending conversations. Twitter makes it easy to participate in conversations by aggregating trending hashtags. Commenting or reading what is trending is a fun way to connect with others who might share the same thoughts as you. Another way to engage with others on Twitter is to mention them in a tweet. Not only will your followers see the tweet, but so will the person you mention.

<u>Instagram</u>

Armed with photos and memes, Instagram users share on a visual level. Like Twitter, Instagram utilizes hashtags to help users categorize their posts with similar posts from other users. Most major brands have an Instagram account – they have learned that the personal level at which they can connect with their consumers is greater on Instagram. Use the search function to find users who share your interests and begin engaging with them. Be sure you share as well. As you share and use hashtags with your share, you will see others reach out to you.

I have made some of the most incredible connections and worthwhile relationships through social media. People I would have never met in real life because miles separated us. We send messages of encouragement and support to each other. I have also been able to turn to the connections I have made strictly online, asking for recommendations and advice.

The internet is not what it used to be. For every five amoral people on the internet, there are fifty moral people. Use your gut. Follow your instinct. But whatever you do, don't shy away from something that can open doors for you in an incredible way.

There are many avenues available for meeting new people. Find which avenue suits your style best and go for it. Do not be afraid of new experiences and opportunities to stretch. **The more you make yourself visible, the more you make it easier for new relationships to be added to your network.**

TAKEAWAYS AND RECAP

- Opportunities to meet new people exist in both reality and online.
- Meetup and Eventbrite are free apps that can be used to discover groups and events.
- Engaging with groups found on social media is a great way to establish credibility.
- Stretch and challenge yourself to attend events, even if it is uncomfortable.

Connect, Build, Grow

Chapter 7: Engaging Strategic Partners

"You can make more friends in two months by becoming interested in other people than you can in two years by trying to get other people interested in you." – Dale Carnegie

Courage has overcome you and you are ready to approach your target. You know why you want to speak with them. You have assessed your presence and know your brand. You have assessed your presentation and know what you have to offer – and it is amazing. The only thing left to do is strike the conversation.

What do you do?

You will be interested in them and you will listen.

"But I just worked hard to nail my elevator speech!" That is wonderful, but once the exchange of hello is made and brief introductions are given you are going to switch from speaking mode to listening mode. Your focus will turn away from you and hone in on the person you are speaking with.

It is estimated that most people spend about 30%-40% of their speaking time talking about themselves. A 2012 research study conducted at the Social Cognitive and Affective Neuroscience Lab at Harvard University discovered that the same parts of the brain that are activated by sex, money, food and drug addiction are activated when people talk about themselves. Diana Tamir, PhD, lead researcher states "Some studies show that the more you self-disclose to someone, the more you like them, the more they like you."[1]

Imagine you are in front of the person you want to build a relationship with. You both introduce yourselves and you then lead in with a question that allows this person to talk about themselves. During this process of them talking about themselves, you inadvertently activate their brain's reward center and make them happy. At the end of the night they go home and recollect scenes from the evening. Whose scene will be brought to memory? Yours. Because you

---

[1] Mitchell, J.P and Tamir, D.I (2012) Disclosing information about the self is intrinsically rewarding. Proceedings of the National Academy of Sciences of the United States, Volume 109 (no. 21), pp 8038-8043. Retrieved: http://psnlab.princeton.edu/sites/default/files/publications-pdf/Tamir-PNAS-2012.pdf

let them talk about themselves you have successfully positioned yourself as a responsible party to their happiness.

It is not as difficult as it seems. In fact, it is fun.

I have met so many interesting people because I have been interested in them, genuinely interested. I recall waiting in a hotel lobby as a conference was about to begin. I struck up a conversation with a gentleman with a drink in his hand – he was the only one with a drink in his hand so he made himself an open target for conversation. After I introduced myself I asked him what he did. He proceeded to tell me. Unfortunately, I cannot recall his title but I recall what he did: he examined manufacturing tools and tool processes. I had never met anyone who did this. Genuinely interested, I asked questions up until the doors of the conference opened. I had a speaking role at this conference but after the event was over he congratulated me and gave me a big hug. In less than 20 minutes I made a connection with this gentleman and I did not offer more than my name.

Listening is one of the greatest challenges to man. The Harvard study confirms the biological reasons as to why. We like feeling good so we naturally do those things that make us feel good. However, the reward we gain from listening is so great. Not because we are making a connection with someone but rather because we are contributing to the happiness of someone else.

Make listening a priority. Practice your listening skills whenever you are given the opportunity. Because this is not something we are often inclined to do, it will take some time to develop the skill. Those who make an effort to listen will inevitably shine more brightly than those who choose to talk all the time.

Knowing what you know now, it might be enticing to "game" the system of human bonding. Don't do it. If you aren't genuinely interested, don't pretend. Politely excuse yourself or go right into sharing. We are fine-tuned to tell if someone is not interested in us. Being insincere can potentially do more harm than good. Although there are those who make a living out of scamming others with charm, most of us do not possess that ability. Don't try it. This might just be an individual you have casual conversation with for that moment, nothing more.

Here is a list of quick conversation starters to help prime you:

Where are you originally from?
How long have you been involved with/worked for this organization?
How did you find out about this organization?
Do you attend these types of events often?
This is my first time attending one of these events, what advice do you have for me?
How has your week been?
Do you have any big plans for the weekend?
Any major vacations on the horizon?

Keep the conversation light and friendly. Unless you are attending a political or religious event, shy away from political or religious topics. Current events are typically okay to discuss but be acutely aware of any topic that could be controversial or divisive. As we discussed in Chapter 4, people want to affiliate themselves with people who are amiable. Unless the other person initiates it, play it safe and stay away from those conversations.

Following up with those you connect with will be your next step. Be sure you know the person's name and can remember something about them that can be referenced in your follow up.

To help you remember their name, make it a point to repeat it several times during the conversation. If someone you know passes by while you two are talking, introduce your new connection by saying their name. If you forget it, you can allow them to say it by introducing themselves. By the end of the night however, know their name.

Actively listening while they speak will help you remember what they say. When we are active listeners, we are focusing on what is being said. We are not listening for the sake of figuring out what to say when it is our turn to speak, we are listening for the sake of hearing the other person's story or point of view. We are appropriately responding with body language that matches the speaker's. We are visualizing what they are saying and responding accordingly.

Of each aspect that is addressed in this guide, this aspect is the <u>most important</u>. Although education and experience are valuable, they don't hold a light to the power of the human spirit.

The ability to connect with someone is one of the most powerful tools we have. Engaging with others can make or break our success. If this part of the process is uncomfortable to you, I encourage you to not give up. It takes practice to become comfortable with engaging others.

When you are beginning to build your network and you attend an event, limit yourself to speaking with no more than 3 people. There is a lot that goes into initiating a bond with someone else. Attempting to bond with more than three people at one event will leave you drained and could prove fruitless. You will eventually create your own gauge for this, so for right now just keep your contacts to a minimum.

As you set out to say "goodbye" or "see you later" remember these two things:

1. Get their contact information as you give them your contact information.
2. Reiterate with them an exact time to expect a follow up from you.

If you are exchanging business cards be sure to look at their card and point something out: company logo, job title, slogan on card, etc. When you take the extra step to point something out on their card you are letting them know that you are not in the business of simply collecting cards, but rather you are in the business of building and collecting meaningful contacts.

With advances in technology, you will attend events where there are no business cards being exchanged. Be sure that your cell phone is fully charged so you do not miss out on an opportunity. Have your social media apps of choice downloaded so you can connect via social media right there, in the moment. If you end up connecting through social media, be sure to send a personalized message to their inbox thanking them for their time.

Be sure you inform them that you will follow up. Set a specific time frame so they are keeping their eyes open for your message or phone call. You will leave quite an impression when you follow through. They will know that you are serious. This will set you apart.

Do not overcomplicate how you engage with others. Remember, your job is to make them remember you, not only because of what you personally bring to the table but rather because of how you made them feel.

People are people regardless of what we associate them with. The CEO of a major company has the same human desires as the drive-through attendant at your restaurant chain of choice. People want to feel valued. Treat everyone with equal compassion, kindness and respect and you will be rewarded.

TAKEAWAYS AND RECAP

- Be genuinely interested in others. Focus on getting to know them.
- When people talk about themselves their brain's reward center is activated.
- Keep conversations light and positive when first meeting someone.
- Actively listen when someone is speaking with you; visualize and empathize.
- Leave with a way to connect and commit to following up.

Chapter 8: Maintaining Your Relationships

"All men are caught in an inescapable network of mutuality." – Dr. Martin Luther King, Jr.

Networking is a continuous cycle. You cannot meet someone one day or connect with someone online and expect that person to be an immediate "go-to". It takes time and effort to build relationships. Just as a garden requires care, so do the relationships you build and place into your network.

The seed is planted upon first meeting. Through emails, text messages or casual conversation, the seed is watered. With compliments, gifts and new connections the seed is given light. Weeds are pulled when we prevent mishaps and follow through with our word. Because of the consideration and care we have given to the relationship, it bears fruit in the form of job opportunity, new contracts, special invitations, access and overall positive experiences.

When a new connection is made, it is of the utmost importance to nourish and nurture it. Your life may be busy but it does not take an unreasonable amount of time to stay connected with your network.

First, determine the amount of attention the relationship is going to need. Some people just need to be contacted once a quarter and will consider themselves a champion of your endeavors. Others need a hello every month. Be savvy and gauge which category your connections fall under.

Next, set aside time to tend regularly check in with your network. Maybe it is the first Monday of each month. On this Monday, you send emails to five people in your network just to say hello, ask them how they are doing and give one to two sentences regarding what you are doing.

Being sensitive to the needs of the relationship and making it a point to stay connected with a certain amount of frequency adds value to the relationship. This sets you apart from most people.

If you really want your network to feel appreciated, nurture them with thoughtfulness. Free event in town? Send a quick message. Have extra tickets to a show? Send an invite. Know of a job opening? Share it. Someone you think they should know? Introduce them. Add value. Make the relationship mutually rewarding and consistently relevant.

Remember that people want to feel a connection. Be that connection. Don't make every touchpoint work related. The small gesture of a simple hello goes a long way.

Given technology today, there is no excuse for letting a relationship fade. Utilize the scheduled email function, just be cautious and keep track of what you have scheduled. Some cell phones have even added the function of scheduling text messages. Leverage social media with a personalized message. There is absolutely no excuse for a gap in communication.

A solid relationship is built over time by making time. If the relationship is important to you, you will make time. Let's commit to making time.

I have created a manifesto to help hold you accountable for the relationships you have and are building. Fill in the blanks and put it into action. Make a photo copy for yourself and place it somewhere as a reminder.

My Networking Manifesto

I am building relationships and growing a solid network. I understand that the relationships in my network must be maintained with consistent, genuine communication. I am dedicated to the maintenance of the relationships and I therefore commit to the following

I will contact at least __ people each month just to say "Hello."

I will be open to many the many ways available for me to connect, however I will utilize _____ (email/text/social media/phone call) most often.

I will leverage technology and add this activity to my cell phone calendar, with a reminder, because it is important to me.

I will be aware of opportunities that I can share with my network and will actively present the opportunities, because I want to add value.

Building my network with meaningful relationships matters to me. Adding value to the relationships in my network matters to me.

I have "go-to" people in my network but I am also a "go-to" person.

This might take time to get used to. It will require changing your perception, but that is what is we have done throughout this entire guide. Celebrate the small steps you take in creating consistent contact and eventually it will become second nature. If you want to make it easier for yourself, focus on the aspect of adding value to others and becoming *their* "go-to." See this as your opportunity to serve, instead of an opportunity to turn on the flashing lights around your profile picture.

TAKEAWAYS AND RECAP

- Relationships and networks must be nourished and nurtured.
- Determine how much care each relationship needs and nurture accordingly.
- Use technology to remind you when to reach out and say hello to members of your network.
- Add value to your relationships by adding perks.
- Celebrate small victories throughout your journey to build solid relationships for your solid network.

Chapter 9: Networking Nuggets

"They will always be a stranger if you don't say hello. They will always be someone you just said hello to if you don't listen." – Ashley René Casey

Networking is nothing more than being intentional with whom we engage and building mutually beneficial relationships.

Here are closing tips to think about before we part:

- People are people regardless of their title, their social status or their educational background; we all just want to feel valued.
- Not every relationship will spark and flourish. Know how and when to sever ties but resist the urge to burn a bridge.
- Add to your network what you take from it. Do not use people – it will catch up to you.
- Just as you do not use people, do not let people use you. Set boundaries and be willing to say no.

Be intentional. Be genuine. Be attentive. Be helpful. Connect. Build. Grow. #yougotthis

About the Author

Ashley René Casey is Owner and CEO of Be Bold and Speak, a communication and leadership coaching and consulting firm committed to helping clients remove barriers so they can share their message more effectively. Her professional experience as a leader at a Fortune 500 company, coupled with her personal experience as lead singer in a rock band has given her a unique perspective on communicating and connecting with others. Ashley René resides in Fort Worth, TX with her two sons and their dog MC Mikey.

Back-Pocket Business Guide Series

Complete your Back-Pocket Business Guide series and invest in these future titles available on Amazon.

Standing at the Front of the Room: Tips to Help You Present with Confidence

In the Meantime: How to Make the Most of Your Current Position Until You Land the Job of Your Dreams

Speak So They Hear You: How to Effectively Communicate Your Message Every Time

I'm Qualified but No One Seems to Notice: How to Strategically Navigate the Job Search Process

Sweating Bullets: Tips to Nail Your Next Interview

For more information on coaching, speaking and training opportunities offered by Ashley René Casey visit www.beboldandspeak.com.

www.ingramcontent.com/pod-product-compliance
Lightning Source LLC
Chambersburg PA
CBHW070103210526
45170CB00012B/731